Defending
the Line

Other books in the Zonderkidz Biography Series

Defending the Line

The David Luiz Story

Alex Carpenter

ZONDER**kidz**

ZONDERKIDZ

Defending the Line
Copyright © 2014 by Alex Carpenter

This title is also available as a Zondervan ebook.
Visit www.zondervan.com/ebooks.

Requests for information should be addressed to:

Zonderkidz, 3900 *Sparks Drive SE, Grand Rapids, Michigan* 49546

978-0310-74641-6

All Scripture quotations, unless otherwise indicated, are taken from The Holy Bible,
New International Version®, NIV®. Copyright © 1973, 1978, 1984, 2011 by Biblica, Inc.®
Used by permission. All rights reserved worldwide.

Any Internet addresses (websites, blogs, etc.) and telephone numbers in this book
are offered as a resource. They are not intended in any way to be or imply an en-
dorsement by Zondervan, nor does Zondervan vouch for the content of these sites
and numbers for the life of this book.

All rights reserved. No part of this publication may be reproduced, stored in a re-
trieval system, or transmitted in any form or by any means—electronic, mechanical,
photocopy, recording, or any other—except for brief quotations in printed reviews,
without the prior permission of the publisher.

Zonderkidz is a trademark of Zondervan.

Cover design: Deborah Washburn
Cover photo: Getty Images
*Interior design: Beth Shagene, Greg Johnson/Textbook Perfect, and Carlos Eluterio
Estrada*

Printed in the United States of America

14 15 16 17 18 /DCI/ 22 21 20 19 18 17 16 15 14 13 12 11 10 9 8 7 6 5 4 3 2 1

Contents

"Everything in life belongs to God.
Our purpose has already been mapped out."
—David Luiz Moreira Marinho

Learning the Lingo for Defending the Line

Acao Social David Luiz: nonprofit charity that David Luiz started

acarajé: a Brazilian dish made of deep-fried black-eyed peas soaked in palm oil

baiano: Portuguese word for native of Bahia

Barradão: Manoel Barradas stadium where Clube Vitória plays

Benfica: football club in Lisbon, Portugal

Brasilia: capital of Brazil

capoeira: a Brazilian dance of African origin that incorporates martial arts movements such as kicks and chops

Chelsea Football Club: soccer team in London, England

Confederations Cup: a tournament organized by FIFA one year before the World Cup, in conjunction with the country that will host the next World Cup

"Deus e fiel": Portuguese for "God is faithful"

Diadema: city in Brazil where David Luiz was born and lived until he was about 14

Estadio da Luz: Portuguese for Stadium of Light

favela: a slum

FIFA: Federation Internationale de Football, association for all international soccer, organizer of the World Cup every four years

futebol de rua: Portuguese word for street soccer

Liga Zon Sagres: soccer league for professional teams in Portugal

luz: Portuguese word for light

Maracanã stadium: soccer stadium in Rio de Janeiro, Brazil

maracanazo: slang Portuguese term for any game upset at Maracanã stadium or of the Brazilian national team

Massa: literally means mass; also a strength and endurance development program for Brazilian youth soccer players

Nordeste: Portuguese for northeast

"O gigante acordou!": Portuguese for "The giant has awoken"

"Ouse ser Brasileiro": Portuguese for "Dare to be Brazilian"

paulista: Portuguese term for someone born in São Paulo

Pelé: legendary soccer player from Brazil, named co-player of the century by FIFA in 1999

peneira: a test for young soccer players in Brazil that filters out the good players from the average ones

"Quer jogar bola?": Portuguese for "Do you want to play ball?"

Relegation: to drop a team from their current level of play to a lower division

Rio de Janeiro: Brazil's second largest city

Seleção: National football team for Brazil that plays in the World Cup and other international championships

Série A, B, C: divisions of Brazilian professional soccer, A is the highest division and C is the lowest

UEFA: governing body for European football

UEFA Champions League: annual international soccer championship for all European football clubs at the top level of professional play

UEFA Europa League: annual international soccer championship for all European football clubs at the lower level of professional play

Vitória: victory, also the short name of Esporte Clube Vitória soccer club in Salvador, Brazil

A Game of Moments

In the country of Brazil, soccer is life. When someone asks, "Quer jogar bola?" (or "Do you want to play ball?") there is no confusion about what sport they mean. Without a doubt, this country, and its intense love of soccer, has dominated the world soccer stage for many years. The Brazilian national squad, or the Seleção, as it is affectionately called, has won the most World Cup championships—five in all. The dominance of the Seleção started all the way back in 1958, the year Brazil won its first World Cup championship title. Four years later, in 1962, Brazil won it again. Then came 1970 and the last hurrah from Pelé, Brazil's (and the world's) greatest soccer player. Two decades later, Brazil gained its fourth title. Then in 2002, Japan and Korea were the stages for Brazil's fifth win.

The Seleção at times seems like it is more than just a

team. Maybe it represents Brazilians' hopes and dreams. But even in this story of dominance, the Seleção has given the Brazilian people its fair share of heartbreaks. Imagine knowing that you are the best team in the world with the best players and then losing to another team that you know you could have (and probably should have) beaten. For the Seleção, Heartbreak Number One was the 1950 loss to Uruguay in the World Cup final. Losing would have been bad enough, but Brazil was the host country for this World Cup. The Maracanã stadium, in Brazil's second largest city of Rio de Janeiro, was filled with 100,000 spectators. But it had never been quieter than on that day in 1950. People all over Brazil, dressed up for the occasion, quietly turned off their radios broadcasting the game. Even the announcers didn't know what else to say. The home fans had been let down by their favorite team in the worst way.

Straffon Images/Xinhua/Landov

Exuberant Brazilian fans cheer on the Seleção at the Maracanã Stadium.

The president of FIFA (international soccer's highest authority) at the time of the Cup, Jules Rimet, was so confident that Brazil would emerge as victors from the game that he had already prepared a postmatch speech in Portuguese to congratulate the Seleção players. Plus, the Brazilian Football Confederation had prepared winners' medals for each of the Brazilian players.

However, Uruguay was not about to squander an opportunity to stun the world. As a member of the elite group of nations that had already won the World Cup in previous years, the Uruguayan team intended to give Brazil a run for their money. In a strategy devised by their manager, Juan López, Uruguay started the game with an offensive attack on the favored Brazilian squad. His decision appeared unwise in the second half when Brazilian forward Friaça gave the hosts a 1–0 lead in the 47th minute. The Maracanã was set ablaze by Friaça's first goal, and a Brazilian victory was just waiting to happen. But then there was the Uruguayan courage and determination. The Uruguayan team's attacks paid off as they tied the game in the 66th minute, with a goal from forward Juan Alberto Schiaffino. The Brazilian fans at the Maracanã were now on the edge of their seats with less than thirty minutes left in the game. If Uruguay scored once more, the dream of a Brazilian lifting the trophy would be over. Uruguay took the lead with a strike from winger Alcides Ghiggia.

FIFA President Rimet said Ghiggia's winning goal had a dramatic effect on the crowd: "The silence was morbid, sometimes too difficult to bear." This was the effect of heartbreak on the devoted fans of the Seleção. To this day, this kind of silence still happens when Brazil is eliminated from the World Cup finals. In the country of soccer, after all, how is it even possible that the Seleção can lose? Nearly 100,000 Brazilian fans couldn't believe that Brazil had come so close yet faltered in the final minutes.

That fateful match in 1950 gave birth to the slang term maracanazo, which Brazilians now say about any upset in the Maracanã stadium of the Brazilian national team or any of the four main Brazilian clubs in Rio de Janeiro (Flamengo, Fluminense, Vasco da Gama, and Botafogo).

When everyone is trying to find an answer to the question "What just happened?" people will turn to unusual practices to place blame on someone or something for the loss. So after the fiasco with Uruguay, the Brazilian national team was so upset that they got rid of their jerseys. They thought their white and blue uniforms were jinxed. So they switched to new colors and a new design—which they still wear today!

Next in the list of heartbreaks was Brazil's loss in the 1982 World Cup to Italy in the tournament hosted by Spain. After beating Argentina with a commanding 3–1 victory, the Seleção was then completely overshadowed by Italy. Brazil fell just short of the semifinals. What was so bad about this loss was the fact that the 1982 Seleção team is hailed by many as the greatest overall squad of players to have ever come together as a Brazilian national team. So that year, Brazil was once again considered the heavy favorite to win the international championship. But that specific Seleção team was never given a second chance to live up to its high expectations.

Throughout the years, many issues have been uncertain in Brazil, such as what kind of president will run the country or how to get rid of so much poverty in the nation. Sadly, there are kids in Brazil who spend their days begging for food at streetlights and sleeping on the streets at night. Despite these difficult circumstances, many Brazilians like to close their eyes at night and be able to sleepily say, "At the end of the day, at least the Seleção is doing well."

So what happens when the Seleção is not doing well? What happens when the people who once loved the team so passionately stop believing that somehow the Seleção will overcome every obstacle in order to win another World Cup championship? What happens, quite simply, are defining moments. And those defining moments occur when players, such as David Luiz Moreira Marinho, bring revival to a team. Now that you have a glimpse of how important soccer is in Brazil, it's time to embark on the story of David Luiz. The opportunity to play a role in the story of Brazilian futebol is one that David Luiz embraced wholeheartedly.

The World Cup Draws Nearer

Every four years, just like the World Cup, a tournament called the Confederations Cup is organized by FIFA in conjunction with the country that will host the next World Cup. For instance, South Africa was to be the 2010 World Cup host country, so they also hosted the 2009 Confederations Cup. In 2009, Brazil narrowly beat the United States in the final match to win the gold medal. Four years later, it was Brazil's turn to host the 2013 Confederations Cup, in preparation for the 2014 World Cup.

After sixty-four years, Brazil was once again going to have the opportunity to host the World Cup on its own soil. In many ways, the Confederations Cup serves as a kind of "practice" for the World Cup, because there are fewer teams that compete (only eight instead of thirty-two teams in the World Cup). Nevertheless, practice or not, every time the Seleção plays, the pressure is on. Furthermore, the Seleção was coming into this tournament under a lot of criticism and scrutiny because of their disappointing showing at the 2012 London Olympics.

The twenty-three-man squad, selected by Seleção coach Luiz Felipe Scolari, was heading into its final tournament before its next chance to bring home another World Cup title. The expectations of a doubtful fan base, combined with a need to impress the world with its usual razzle-dazzle, increased the pressure on each one of the Brazilian players. However, beyond the lines of the soccer field, something more serious than soccer was going on in Brazil.

For many years, soccer had been the most important thing about Brazilian life. In 2013, many Brazilians now felt like soccer alone couldn't ease their troubles. When the Confederations Cup came to Brazil in the summer of 2013, the Brazilians were not very happy. They loved soccer, but they didn't want their government spending a lot of money on a big sporting event when poor people in their country needed help. This frustration led to protests all over Brazil, many of them taking place just blocks away from the stadiums that would host the Confederations Cup.

In light of these protests, many of the Seleção players dedicated their play in the Confederations Cup to the people of Brazil. A popular slogan during this time was, "O gigante acordou!" or "The giant has awoken!" referring to Brazil as the giant that was now ready to confront its own problems. Players, such as David Luiz Moreira

Marinho, a tall, big-haired defender with tons of personality who'd grown up in the modest city of Diadema in São Paulo, vowed to play the tournament on behalf

David's boyhood dreams came true when he put on the No. 4 jersey as part of the Seleção.

of the Brazilian people who had finally decided to stand up against corruption.

David Luiz (pronounced DAH-veed LOO-eez) would later go on to save the Seleção in the Confederations Cup, living up to his promise of playing with his whole heart for the people he loved. But before David Luiz's great moments in the 2013 Confederations Cup, proudly sporting the No. 4 jersey for the Seleção, he was simply David, a boy from a city on the outskirts of the sprawling metropolis of São Paulo. He was just a boy with a big heart and personality to spare, dreaming of one day becoming a professional soccer player.

David from Diadema

Soccer, like any sport, is made of moments. Some moments lead to wild celebration, the hopes of thousands of fans fulfilled in one single act of athletic heroism. Other moments, however, lead to disappointment, symbolized in the unbelieving faces of a once hopeful crowd. In these moments, though, it's not always about winning or losing.

Any champion, like David Luiz, will tell you that losing is part of being an athlete. What defines you, what really defines you, is your character. This is David Luiz's story of being an athlete whose highlight reel is about hard work and endurance.

David Luiz was born and raised in the city of Diadema, which is about ten miles outside of the huge city of São Paulo, one of the world's top ten largest cities (its greater metropolitan area consists of almost 20 million people). Diadema itself is a city full of hard workers.

The people there prize family values more than wealth. In some ways, Diadema is like São Paulo but smaller. The buildings and homes look the same. They have the same kinds of markets and shops, though kids may walk to school instead of facing the crazy São Paulo traffic jams. Yet, with a population of 390,000 people, Diadema is not a small town.

Diadema is home to a butterfly zoo and an observatory, the kinds of attractions that any kid in the States might visit for a school field trip. In the city where David Luiz grew up, there are no fancy malls, no theme parks, no laser tag facilities. But growing up in a place where people valued hard work would play a significant role in the direction that David Luiz's life would take.

He was a typical Brazilian kid from a modest family who made up for lack of money with an abundance of joy. His parents, Regina Célia and Ladislau Marinho, supported him in all he did, giving him a nurturing home. While the food and the language are different in Brazil, many of the values are the same as in the United States.

To the outside world, Brazil is known for its samba music, vivid colors, and its natural wonders, such as the Amazon rainforest and Iguaçu falls. And without a doubt, Brazil is a country defined by soccer.

The following saying about soccer in Brazil was coined by one of Brazil's great writers: "We are passionate about soccer because it is played by mere human beings." In other words, soccer is so important because people, just like you and me, are in charge of the outcome of the game. In the final seconds of a soccer game, if two teams are tied, one player could make all the difference with a kick from outside the box.

Before the eventual success David Luiz found on the soccer field, he was simply a skinny kid from Diadema who wanted to play soccer every day just like all the other kids. Every kid in Brazil knows something about soccer. Every family has a favorite team. Every kid has a favorite player. Soccer is the sport; it's what everybody does for exercise and fun—no matter where.

In the favelas, or slums, kids are lucky if they have their own ball to play with because very few families can afford anything more than the bare necessities. But they still play soccer—in the streets. From one minute to the next, the streets change from a place where cars drive by to an improvised soccer field.

David Luiz has been playing and practicing his soccer moves since he was a young boy in Diadema.

Brazil is in love with its sport, with its soccer heroes, but it's also a country that needs so much more than just wins on the soccer field. It's a country filled with people who demonstrate joy and grit, people who smile in spite of life's difficulties.

This is the country that David Luiz comes from, and it's the country he loves to give back to.

The Peneira

With every kick while playing futebol de rua, or street soccer, David Luiz dreamed about becoming a pro soccer player some day. The more he played, the more he realized that he might have a chance. His natural talent, combined with his never-ending hustle, made him stand out on the field.

Then one day, when David Luiz was about twelve years old, he decided to go to the peneira tryouts for soccer.

To any Brazilian kid dreaming of playing professional soccer some day, the peneira is like one big test day. The peneira is the ultimate dividing line between those who will only dream of playing on their favorite soccer squad and those who will actually have the honor of playing soccer as a professional. The Portuguese word peneira actually refers to a sieve, which is a mesh tool that sifts out large from small items. With soccer, the peneira selects the best players in a group and filters out the rest. Thousands of Brazilian boys dream of entering this human filter. A few are selected as recruits. The others are tossed out as unwanted. This is the real experience of the peneira for boys with big dreams, each one no more than fourteen or fifteen years of age.

Imagine waking up at 6:00 a.m. to catch a bus that will take you to a training center an hour away from your own home, to a city or neighborhood that you have only heard about. As you step onto the bus, you notice another twenty freshly groomed teenagers, each looking just as nervous and anxious as you do. This rented bus will take the group out into the Brazilian countryside. Maybe some of the boys speak quietly to each other, but most sit nervously in silence. This day will end with either a shattered or accomplished dream for each boy. Every major professional soccer club in Brazil holds peneiras, some up to four times a week in search of the next wave of soccer talent. According to Brazilian agent Cláudio Sparapani, who helps scout talent for soccer clubs, for every 1,000 kids tested, only one is likely to move into the ranks of the club team.

These buses will bring in at least fifty young players from around the city to a specific club team peneira. If a player doesn't make the cut for one team's peneira, he can always try again elsewhere. But with the odds nearly impossible, a young player has to truly believe in himself.

Between skill drills and scrimmages, scouts from

club teams will use the peneira to recruit players for their youth squads. For many, the peneira experience is the ultimate reality check. Someone who may have been the best soccer player on their street may pale in comparison to the top players at the peneira.

In the intensely competitive world of Brazilian professional soccer, there is little to no room for error. With millions of boys playing every single day, whether in the streets or on grass fields, only a very few will ever make it to the world stage, let alone to the national stage.

One of the scouts saw something in David Luiz and recruited him to be a part of the youth team for São Paulo Futebol Clube, one of the most prestigious club teams in Brazil, the six-time League winner (the most of any Brazilian team) and three-time FIFA World Club Championship winner (again, the most of any Brazilian team). This was the glimmer of hope that David Luiz needed, the affirmation that he did in fact possess some real talent in the game of soccer, even with the odds stacked against him at the peneira. In a haystack of a thousand players, David Luiz was looking to be the one kid with enough talent that could someday translate into success on the field with the pros.

Despite the fierce competition of other Brazilian boys who had played soccer every day of their lives too, now David Luiz had a spot on the São Paulo youth squad. This was a foot in the door, an opportunity to make his soccer dreams come true. David Luiz made his best efforts to prove himself at São Paulo. But he ended up being released from the São Paulo squad after training with them for two years. While the coaching staff at São Paulo had recognized talent in him, the coaches saw David Luiz as physically fragile, too scrawny to thrive in the big leagues.

His visions of wearing the São Paulo jersey were crushed. But his dreams weren't over. They would just move to a new location, a whole new home—the city of Salvador, in the northeastern state of Bahia. But with his family living in Diadema, David Luiz would have to make the trek to Bahia alone, away from his family and childhood friends.

Moving to Salvador

Fortunately, a scout from Esporte Clube Vitória, an elite team from Bahia, had seen David Luiz's ability at a peneira in Diadema. While Vitória was a step down in terms of prestige, this club still offered opportunity to a young player. Away from his family at only fourteen, David Luiz had to go to school in a new city, studying without his parents close by to help him. He would have to trust God to be with him on this new journey.

Esporte Clube Vitória, usually known simply as Vitória, or "Victory," was founded on May 13, 1899, in the city of Salvador. Vitória's home games are played at the club's stadium, Manoel Barradas (known as the Barradão to locals). The team mascot is a lion, a symbol of the fierce passion of the people of Bahia. The professional side of Vitória had limited success. The team had never won a national league title. But the youth squad of the club is one of the most successful of the world.

Between 1995 and 2000, at its peak, the youth team held at least twenty-one international titles. Players such as Bebeto, Dida, and Júnior (all later Brazilian World Cup players), are among the caliber of players who started their careers playing for Vitória. David Luiz was joining a club with a history of exporting players to some of the top clubs in Brazil and Europe. While the prospect of playing for Vitória was appealing in many ways, David Luiz was going to have to adjust to a new way of life.

For a city boy who grew up on the outskirts of one of the biggest cities in the world, a move to Salvador as a teenager would mean a drastic change. Imagine living your whole life just outside of New York City and then suddenly moving, on your own, to a town in Texas. Although these cities are both in the United States, they are very different. That's how different Salvador was from Diadema.

For this Diadema boy, the everyday routines and customs of being a paulista (the term for someone born in the state of São Paulo), were now being replaced by the baiano way of life. The food was different, the accent was different, the sights and sounds were different. In Bahia, for example, one of the local delicacies is acarajé, a dish made of deep-fried black-eyed peas soaked in palm oil. In Diadema, it's unlikely that David Luiz would have ever eaten this, much less seen it. Known more for capoeira, a martial art created by African slaves about

400 years ago, the state of Bahia represents a different culture within Brazil.

Here, in the heart of the Nordeste (in Portuguese, simply "the Northeast"), David Luiz would mature as a player and as a young man. One thing remained the same: David Luiz loved soccer, and soccer had now taken him to Salvador. His dedication to the game would soon be the defining aspect of his life in Salvador. Vitória would provide him with the best victories of his career as a young athlete.

David Luiz has been playing professional club soccer for more than half of his life.

David Luiz was well aware of the fact that even riding the bench as a teen for a professional team in Brazil meant that he was overcoming the odds. David Luiz had been given a second chance to shine on a Brazilian soccer team. But he had to work hard and persevere.

The coaches had approved David Luiz in the initial tryouts with Vitória, but there was not any guarantee that he would play as a regular member of the youth squad. In tryouts, David Luiz played as a defensive midfielder. The typical image of someone playing in this position is that of a strong, able-bodied player, who can use physical strength to gain an advantage on the field. Throughout the history of the game, defensive midfielders have been known as sheriffs or bulldogs. Many end up wearing the captain's armband due to their no-nonsense style of leadership on the field.

Based on his experience with the São Paulo team, David Luiz knew he was considered by many to be too skinny. João Paulo Sampaio, one of the key members of the Vitória coaching staff at the time, remembers his early days working with David Luiz: "He was very tall and very green as a player. He was still in a phase of physical development, in which his bones were still growing at a faster rate than his [muscles]." Again, David Luiz was hearing the same critique but it had little to do with actual playing ability.

To develop David Luiz's bulk and strength, the coaching staff entered him into a strength and conditioning program at Vitória called Massa. The goal was to develop players in the youth squad to prepare them for professional play. A select group of young players would take part in nutrition and exercise-based activities for about six months. The hope was that this program would strengthen each athlete's endurance and physical toughness, while training them to protect themselves from injury. As a defensive player, David Luiz needed Massa training. However, he would have to pay close attention to the people who were willing to invest in him and be patient. The Massa program was so demanding that its participants rarely played in actual games.

At the conclusion of Massa, David Luiz emerged as a stronger player. Again, Sampaio recalls: "David Luiz started playing as a central defender and started to participate more regularly in our game preparation. He gained thirteen to seventeen pounds." Now, the tall, scrawny kid from Diadema was ready to contribute to the Vitória youth squad in a more significant way.

Now, as David Luiz looks back at his time with Vitória, he remembers how good it was for him: "I have very good memories and friends there, the place where I was given the chance to become a professional soccer player. Vitória is a great soccer club, and I have great memories of my time there."

His humble beginnings in Diadema, playing soccer with his friends and neighbors in hopes that someday he might get noticed for his skill and ability, had developed his character. He was now being forced into maturity by simply having to endure challenging training and criticism, right after he had to make the move to Salvador without his family. When he was let go from São Paulo's youth team, he didn't give up. Instead, he waited to embrace another opportunity to grow. His own character, coupled with the investment of coaches like Sampaio, enabled him to keep working to become a better player. As David Luiz would start to see, this was preparation for the next chapter of his life—the first chapter of his life in Europe.

Redemption for Vitória

International soccer carries a rule that most other sports don't follow. Every professional team starts the season in their own national league with the possibility of facing something that no fan or player ever wants to happen: relegation. Relegation is a process that forces the lowest-performing teams in the national league to spend the next season competing on a lower level. The lowest teams drop down, and the top performing teams from the lower divisions are promoted into the next level up.

In American sports, it would be like the New York Yankees, the Los Angeles Lakers, or the Dallas Cowboys actually running the risk of having to play in a minor league. Just imagine the Los Angeles Lakers playing in a small town arena, to a packed crowd of five thousand people for a full season!

In Brazil, even the most elite teams have had to

endure the humiliation of relegation. Teams such as Corinthians, Palmeiras, and Botafogo, all previous winners of the Brazilian national league, have been knocked down to the lower division, known as the Série B.

To make a long story short, if you're playing in the Série B, you're less likely to be noticed by a coach for a prestigious team. If you're playing in the Série C, one level below the lower division, your chances of being noticed decrease even more. The Vitória squad was on the lowest level. But not for long. In what can only be described as a God-ordained chain of events, David Luiz was scooped out of anonymity while playing in this Série C league.

As a member of the winning squad of the statewide Bahia youth tournament, at the age of eighteen, David Luiz caught the attention of the professional squad's coach, a former player by the name of Arthurzinho. Arthurzinho recalls his early experiences watching David Luiz play: "He demonstrated a lot of power and stamina, along with a ton of personality for an eighteen-year-old kid. I saw that he was a quality player, so I invited him to join the professional squad, and he ended up doing very well." This had been the chance David Luiz had been waiting for, ever since his first experience at the peneira in his hometown.

Now, as a member of Vitória's professional roster, David Luiz would face the challenge of helping the team climb its way back to the higher divisions of play. Struggling to regain its fame and glory, Vitória would need at least two years to get back to Brazil's elite league.

Aside from its troubles on the field, Vitória also faced its fair share of troubles off the field. The club was deep in a mountain of debt. Unable to bring in players that required high salaries, Vitória was forced to recruit talent from its youth teams.

In the 2006 season, motivated to bring Vitória back to where it belonged, the team, led by Arthurzinho, ended up in second place in the Série C. That meant that they would be promoted to Série B next season. David Luiz was one of Vitória's starters throughout the course of the season. He played as a central defender alongside Wallace and Anderson Martins, two defenders who would later gain greater fame by transferring to other elite clubs in Brazil. The "Lion" from Salvador had woken up, and David Luiz had played a key role in revitalizing a club that desperately needed it.

Sometimes, an athlete's greatest achievements are not measured in medals or paychecks, but in how a situation helped develop and instill character. David Luiz fought alongside his Vitória teammates to improve their team. It may not have been as glamorous as a World Cup game or even an elite Brazilian league matchup, but the matches David Luiz played with Vitória established a foundation for the kind of athlete he would later be when the stakes were a lot higher.

From Vitória to Europe

David Luiz played his hardest. Every game was a new opportunity to demonstrate both his talent on the pitch and his persistent loyalty to the Vitória fans no matter what league Vitória was playing in. His talent attracted club Anderlecht in Belgium to come take a closer look at his game. In the short time when Anderlecht had its sights on David Luiz, however, he didn't deliver the kind of performances they wanted to see. But David Luiz was still young and another European team would come knocking again and soon. Playing in Europe meant a higher salary and higher visibility to the greatest teams in the world.

Three months after Anderlecht backed away from signing him, he would attract the attention of one of Portugal's top clubs, Benfica. Something about this player, this tenacious kid from Diadema, stood out to the management at Benfica, who decided to take a chance on him.

At first, Benfica signed David Luiz with a temporary "loan" contract. That meant he could return to Vitória after several months if things didn't work out in Portugal. At the young age of twenty, David Luiz had signed his first contract with a European soccer club. Now, the Diadema boy would have to prove himself worthy of the opportunity. He would no longer be playing games in the lower-quality stadiums of the Série C teams in Brazil. Rather, he had just joined a squad that would be playing in the UEFA Champions League. For national teams, the World Cup is the most important tournament, the epitome of the soccer world. But for professional club teams, the UEFA Champions League is one of the most important. To say the least, this was far from the modest streets of his Diadema neighborhood.

David shakes hands with the president of Benfica during a press conference in February 2007.

Benfica is a team full of history. Its place in European soccer is among some of the best teams in the world. Founded in 1904, Benfica is Lisbon's most successful club. Most of their successes in the 1960s were achieved with one of the greatest players ever to have played the game, Eusébio. Eusébio's legacy lives on to this day among soccer fans everywhere. During his time at the club in the 1960s, Benfica won eight Portuguese Championships, three Portuguese Cups (1961, '64, and '69), and two European Champions Cups. At one point in time, Benfica could have been considered the best team in Europe, if not the world. This was, in other words, a club full of history, tradition, and expectations. The boy from Diadema was joining the ranks of many players who had played at the highest levels of soccer.

Unfortunately, David Luiz's first exposure to the pressures of European competition was not the debut he had played out in his mind. In a game against French club Paris Saint-Germain, David Luiz was substituting for fellow Brazilian and Benfica idol Luisão. Then David Luiz made a crucial mistake in Paris Saint-Germain's first goal—he was out of position at the wrong time, playing his own unintentional role in the opposing team's tying goal. At half time, David Luiz had a choice: either he could let his nerves get the best of him, or he could keep his head and prove himself to the Benfica fans.

"During the half-time break," he remembers, "I asked God to give me peace, so that I could demonstrate all the hard work and effort I was putting in." If his experiences in soccer had taught him anything, it was that lost games were just another opportunity to try again and to correct his mistakes the next time around.

"In the second half, I played very well," David Luiz recalls. "I proved my worth as a player, and from that point on, I played in every match for the rest of the season." More than gaining the trust of the Benfica fans, he had developed more confidence in himself. "While match day against Paris Saint-Germain had been full of surprises, I had become a stronger person," he said.

Luiz was becoming the kind of player (and person) who embraced life's challenges and made the choice to let faith drive his decisions. David Luiz relied on faith to help him on the field and to adjust to life in Portugal. Once again he was on his own. Far from his family and friends, David Luiz had to adapt to European soccer and culture with only God by his side. And he wasn't about to give up.

After the tumultuous start in a Champions League game against Paris Saint-Germain, David Luiz now made his debut in the local Portuguese league, against the modest União de Leiria. This match would be the first of many—eighty-two in total—that he played wearing the Benfica jersey. The more he played, the more trust he earned from his team, his coaches, and their fans.

At the end of his first season with Benfica, David Luiz signed a five-year deal with the club. The boy from Diadema had finally accomplished what so many other Brazilian boys would only dream of doing: he had signed a long-term contract with a professional European club team. Signing that first contract was an exclamation point after so many years of working hard to earn his place on the teams for which he played.

The New Sheriff in Lisbon

If you were to watch a professional soccer match from the sidelines, you would see eleven players on each team following the ball and their opponents with a great level of attention. If you then closed your eyes, you would hear certain voices frequently throughout the match. One voice you would hear would be that of the goalkeeper. He organizes his defenders and alerts his team members about unmarked opponents. Another strong voice would be the team captain's, orienting his team at every crucial moment. But the voice that might stand out the most is that of the sweeper, or the "sheriff" on the team. So why is this position on the field compared to a sheriff? Unlike the Wild West, there's no need to save the day in a saloon or run some out-of-town bandits away from the city. In soccer, being a central defender requires leadership. A defender must often sacrifice his own body, getting hit by a rocket blast of the ball or an unintentional high kick from an opponent trying to score. In other words, the central defender is like a sheriff because he must have the ability to do something that others may not be brave enough to do.

David Luiz (Benfica) and Emerson (Beira Mar) during the Portuguese Bwin League match between Beira Mar and SL Benfica, in Aveiro, Portugal on April, 9, 2007.

Having gone through the peneira as a young teenager, David Luiz had developed bravery and persistence. When he had to leave his home in Diadema, he had to trust that God would take care of him. When he had to put his playing on hold in order to develop more muscle through the Massa program with Vitória, he was patient, worked hard in practice, and believed that God was in control of his future. David Luiz was ready for the challenge of taking on a new role in Lisbon, one that would require a strong voice and a tenacious attitude. David Luiz was now a "sheriff" for Benfica.

During the course of David Luiz's next year with Benfica, he would have plenty of moments to show just what he was made of, even in games that Benfica didn't win. On November 27, 2008, Benfica was up against

Greek team Olympiacos during a match played in the group stages of the UEFA Champions League. The Greek home crowd was buzzing with anticipation before the game, eager to see if their team could pull off a win against one of Portugal's top teams. Between chants and cheers, David Luiz knew that this was going to be a big game.

After the players stepped onto the field and shook hands, however, things did not go as he had hoped. The tone for the evening was set in the opening minute of the game, when Luciano Galletti, the dangerous right-winger from Argentina, scored a goal. The crowd went wild. By the 24th minute, Christos Patsatzoglou and Brazilian forward Diogo had put Olympiacos up by an additional two goals, making the score now 3–0. In soccer, this kind of a score is often enough to make the losing side throw in the towel. Three goals is a mountain to climb, especially when you're losing on the other team's home field.

But David Luiz was determined not to give up.

Toward the end of the first half, David Luiz scored for the very first time for Benfica. After a corner kick cross into the penalty box, David Luiz volleyed the ball into the back of the net. He was in the right place at the right time. He celebrated his goal in an effort to show his teammates that there was still hope. Throughout the rest of the game, David chased the players he was guarding up and down the field, his hustle relentless and never ending. Even as Olympiacos scored two more goals, David kept trying to win back the ball for Benfica. At the end of the game, the score a dismal 5–1 in favor of Olympiacos, David Luiz had embraced his role as the sheriff in the Benfica back line.

David Luiz Trademarks

1. Defender with Offensive Danger
   While David is a sheriff in the defensive line, he also has a knack for making effective runs up the field. He also takes free kicks, which has allowed him to score goals.

2. He's Got Heart
   For ninety minutes, every game, his passion is clearly evident. He will never give up, no matter what kind of a game he's having.

3. Keeping It Fun
   David Luiz often plays with a smile on his face. He loves the sport, and it shows.

4. The 'Do
   You can't miss David Luiz on the field simply because his hair is so big. His curly fro has become his trademark look.

5. His Faith
   At every opportunity, in all kinds of interviews, David brings up the fact that his life belongs to God. He believes God is in control of everything that happens to him, and that everything he has is a blessing.

Luiz in the Luz

The Portuguese word for light is luz. David Luiz had known this term ever since he was a young child, asking his mother to turn on the luz in the hallway or wondering where the luz had gone after an unexpected power outage in Diadema. This same word would take on a new meaning for David Luiz at Benfica. David Luiz, the new defensive sheriff in the Benfica back line, would be playing (and dominating) every week at Benfica's home stadium, the Estadio da Luz, or Stadium of the Light.

Originally, the stadium got its name because it was situated in a part of town called Luz, in honor of a local Catholic church called Igreja de Nossa Senhora da Luz. But then the stadium's designers actually wanted to incorporate the idea of light into the stadium itself. The roof of the arena allows for natural light to shine down on the field, giving players and the fans alike the experience that they are playing in the light. But even before David Luiz ever stepped foot in the Benfica home arena, he was already well aware of the meaning of the word. In more ways than one, David Luiz would be playing "in the light."

While many other professional athletes were reveling in their own glories and their own talents, David Luiz had chosen to glorify God with his athletic abilities. He knew that all of his success as a player was due to God's plan in his life. Beneath his Benfica jersey, he would often wear a T-shirt that read, "Deus e fiel" or "God is faithful." He was not ashamed to express his faith in God. He was not ashamed to be the kind of "luz" that he believed he needed to be in Portugal.

As he started to shine more and more as a Benfica player, the local media in Lisbon started to take an interest in David Luiz. After all, who was David Luiz? When he had first arrived in Lisbon, a single Benfica employee was the only person to greet David Luiz. He did not receive a big welcome or glamorous reception from a large group of soccer fans. But now he had become one of the starting eleven players for Benfica, one of Portugal's most elite clubs.

"I think that God's plan for my life is very big," David Luiz said in an interview for a Lisbon-based television show. "My job is to try to figure out what that plan is, day by day." More than fame or glory, David Luiz was interested in playing soccer as an act of gratitude for all that God had done in his life.

One of David Luiz's greatest role models is a Brazilian

player who wanted to openly share his Christian faith with the world—Kaká. Kaká, or Ricardo Izecson dos Santos Leite, has played in three World Cups, including

Brazil's win in 2002 for its fifth title. As a member of Italian team AC Milan, Kaká was voted the FIFA Player of the Year in 2007, which meant that at that time he was considered the best soccer player in the world.

David Luiz and his role model Kaká share the field as members of the Seleção.

Having won every kind of title a player could possibly win, Kaká remained a shining example. Beneath his jersey he wore a T-shirt with the words, "I belong to Jesus" proudly stamped on it. Later, Kaká and David Luiz would even have the chance to share the field as members of the Seleção when David Luiz got his first invitation to the team in the summer of 2010.

Picture a basketball player pointing to the sky after making a buzzer-beating shot in the fourth quarter. Or think of an NFL player thanking God after a great showing in a game. Whatever the sport is, many athletes choose to give credit to God in some way. But who really walks the walk of faith? Which of these athletes does more than quickly point to the sky or make a brief mention of God?

In David Luiz's words, "I've learned that in life

we have to put our faith in something. But God never changes, no matter who you are."

"Instead of beating your chest and saying 'I'm the best,' I prefer to thank God," he said. The more he played with the red Benfica jersey on, clearing loose balls or heading balls out of danger, David Luiz kept God in mind. He was where he was because God had put him there, and the time had come for him to be a champion.

Shaun Botterill/Getty Images

David Luiz (here playing for Chelsea) gives God the credit both on and off the field.

Heart of a Champion

Millions of young soccer players around the world run onto a field every day. Somewhere in South Africa, the host country of the 2010 World Cup, for instance, ten boys run onto a field in the poverty-stricken area known as Soweto, dividing themselves into two teams of five. Meanwhile, in the United States, summer soccer camps take place in the American Midwest, and young players run their hearts out on a hot day. More than ever, soccer is the world's game. And every one of these players, boy or girl, second grader or twelfth grader, wants one thing: to win. Every player wants the chance to be a champion. David Luiz was no different.

The Portuguese league, known as the Liga Zon Sagres, holds a tournament every year between sixteen of Portugal's top teams. The first edition of the tournament was held in 1934. Since then only five teams have ever lifted the championship trophy. Unlike most American sports, the league doesn't lead up to any kind of play-off. Instead, every team plays every other team twice throughout the league (once at home and once away). The team with the best record at the end is the league champion. Benfica, with thirty-two titles, has won the league tournament more than any other Portuguese club.

The Benfica fans were used to winning and usually only had to contend with rivals Porto and Sporting for the top spot in the nation. This was the kind of expectation that David Luiz faced as the new sheriff in town. He was ready.

In the league opener, David Luiz was among the starting eleven players against CS Maritimo. After ninety minutes, Benfica ended up tying 1–1 even though Maritimo was a much weaker side. One game down. Twenty-nine more to go. This was going to be a long, grueling season. Through his grit and determination, David Luiz was focused on having a great season with Benfica.

Along with the Portuguese League, however, Benfica also had to compete at a high level in the UEFA Europa League. This tournament is played between the second tier of top teams in Europe, just behind the clubs who qualify for the Champions League. Here was an opportunity for David Luiz to stand out, not only on Portuguese soil, but also on the European stage, in a tournament followed by millions of soccer fans around the world.

David Luiz was part of an organization that had made history so many times. He was no longer just a boy in Diadema watching European soccer on a Saturday morning or a rising star with Vitória wondering if he would ever play ball in Europe. He was now a main character about to embrace his role with the same kind of grit that he had grown used to showing.

The next game was the first of seven consecutive league wins for Benfica. This match, an away game against Vitória Guimaraes, was won at the very end of the game with a late goal by Brazilian midfielder Ramires. The next game, however, was a sign of what was to come for Benfica for the 2009–2010 season. Vitória Setubal, a modest club from the city of Setubal, could do nothing more than watch the magic of the Benfica team firing on all cylinders. The final score: 8–1 in Benfica's favor. With the offense now clicking in all kinds of ways, David Luiz was confident that he could keep the defense on lockdown. David Luiz's confidence—as well as the rest of the team's—began to soar.

For the first nineteen rounds of the Liga Zon Sagres, Benfica went back and forth between first and second place. In the 20th round, Benfica seized first place, determined to finish first and claim the league title. On February 3, 2010, David Luiz and the rest of the Benfica squad played before a home crowd. Luiz, along with his defensive team members, helped Benfica keep their own goal on lockdown. The result: a 3–0 shutout against Uniao Leiria. But the best was yet to come.

In the last game of the season, against Rio Ave, Benfica still had the possibility of letting the trophy slip between their fingers and into the hands of a very capable

Braga squad, which was in second place. On May 9, 2010, the Estadio da Luz was filled to capacity with over 64,000 supporters cheering the home team on, ready to see Benfica claim its 32nd national title. Anticipation was everywhere.

Marcos Borga/Reuters/Landov

David carries the trophy after beating Rio Ave and winning the Portuguese Premier League title.

Now, if you've never had the chance to see a full stadium in a European soccer league, here's what you see: fans from all over the city have their team's scarf draped around their necks. You see flags and banners. You hear all kinds of cheers and chants, specifically for the team being supported.

After only three minutes, Paraguayan star forward Oscar Cardozo put Benfica on the scoreboard. With a powerful left foot volley kick, Benfica was up, 1–0, sending the Estadio da Luz into a frenzy. While Rio Ave would try to spoil the Benfica party with a tying goal from Ricardo Chaves in the 71st minute, this was Benfica's day. After a corner kick taken by Argentinean midfielder Pablo Aimar, Cardozo booted the ball into the back of the net again. This goal guaranteed Benfica's 32nd Portuguese league title and gave David Luiz his first taste of being a European champion.

After the match was over, David Luiz embraced his

teammates in sheer joy, celebrating all of their hard work. When he had congratulated his teammates, he ran over to the stands and celebrated with the fans, an act of thanks for the support they had shown the team throughout the season. The shirt he was wearing was a simple, white V-neck T-shirt, with the words "Deus e fiel" ("God is faithful") written in marker. These were his own words, his own beliefs, proclaimed on his own clothing in a moment when he could have claimed all the glory and merit for himself. He showed his allegiance to God.

With every game that Benfica played throughout the season, David Luiz attracted even more attention to his tenacious style of play. Never giving up, not even for a second, fighting for his teammates and giving God all of the glory for his accomplishments, David Luiz from Diadema had attracted the attention of the great teams of Europe.

In what was one of the greatest moments of his career, David Luiz received an honor that even in his wildest dreams he could never have imagined. In a sport dominated by great midfielders and goal scorers—the guys that add pizzazz and flair to the game—David Luiz was elected Player of the Year for the Portuguese League for the 2009–2010 season. This was a rare honor for a defensive player. That's how valuable David Luiz was to his team. His inability to give up, combined with his humble approach to the game, ended up speaking loudest. Here he was, at twenty-three, winning the most prestigious award in Portuguese soccer.

Seleção Bound

At the end of the European soccer leagues' seasons in May 2010, the world turned its attention elsewhere. The occasion was nothing less than the World Cup, where the top thirty-two nations would face off in South Africa. This was bigger than the NBA Finals, bigger than the World Series, bigger than the Super Bowl. For the final match of the tournament, over 3 billion people tuned in to watch. That's almost half the world's population watching the same thing at the exact same time in different countries and time zones around the globe!

To every soccer fan and player, winning a World Cup for your country is the highest achievement possible. And back in David Luiz's home country of Brazil, expectations were high. Any Brazilian will tell you that whenever Brazil is in the World Cup, there is always a

chance that Brazil will walk away with the championship trophy.

Some fans believed that David Luiz should have been
called up to the Seleção to play for his country. But at the
time, the Brazilian back line was considered one of the
best in the world. Between goalkeeper Julio Cesar, right
back Maicon, and central defender Lucio, who were all
teammates then with Italian team Inter Milan, many
saw the Brazilian defense as an impenetrable wall. Thus,
it was not yet David Luiz's time to play for the Seleção.

What ended up happening to the Seleção broke the
hearts of millions of Brazilians. The Seleção lost 2 – 1 in
the quarterfinals to the Netherlands. Brazilian fans had
to wait another four years for another opportunity to
win their sixth World Cup title.

Do you remember how Brazilian fans and players take
drastic actions after a major loss? What the Brazilian
Soccer Federation ended up doing to respond to this disappointment was to fire the head coach right after the
World Cup. After all, in Brazilian soccer, there are only
two options: win or win. Since the coach had left South
Africa without a trophy, he was replaced. After some de-
liberation, the Brazilian Soccer Federation hired former
Corinthians coach Mano Menezes for the job.

Having barely recovered from the heartbreak of the
South Africa World Cup, Mano Menezes' first job was
to announce the players he had chosen for the new-
est Seleção squad. The team was scheduled to play a
friendly match against the United States in the newly in-
augurated New Meadowlands stadium, where the New

York Giants usually play football during the NFL season. Dressed in a gray suit, no smile or hint of emotion on his face, Menezes began the roster announcement by saying, "The following list will go in alphabetical order."

Here was a chance for the new Seleção coach to reinvent the team, to rescue the magic and mystique of one of the greatest teams in the history of organized sports. He began reading off the names he had selected, name first, then field position, then team name: "Alexandre Pato, forward, AC Milan; Andre, forward, Santos; Andre Santos, left back, Fenerbahce; Carlos Eduardo, midfielder, Hoffenheim; Daniel Alves, right back, Barcelona; David Luiz, central defender, Benfica ..."

Menezes offered David Luiz his first invitation to join the team that had captured David Luiz's heart as a young boy. The list went on, until all of the players had been announced. After the 2010 World Cup loss in South Africa, Menezes' job was to rebuild the team, and he left many veteran players off the squad, including Kaká. But one thing was certain: David Luiz had just accomplished a lifelong dream to be called up to play for his country. He would get to wear the yellow and green jersey that he had worn in his dreams as a young boy playing street ball.

As David Luiz recalls finding out the news, he remembers driving with his friend Gustavo and getting a call from his manager. "My manager told me that I had been invited to play for the Seleção," he says. "Right there and then I stopped the car, just taking in the emotions of the moment, my childhood flashing by in my mind."

Ray Stubblebine/Reuters/Landov

Brazil's David Luiz fights for the ball with United States' Alejandro Bedoya during the first half of their international friendly soccer match.

Less than a month later, on August 8, 2010, David Luiz stepped onto the New Meadowlands playing field, ready to prove that he had deserved the invitation to represent his country. He stood tall, clad in the traditional Seleção uniform, yellow jerseys with green details and blue shorts, the No. 4 stamped on the back of his jersey. The game ended 2–0 in Brazil's favor, goals by then rising star Neymar and Alexandre Pato. David Luiz had played his part in making sure that nobody breached the Brazilian defense. This was only the beginning of David Luiz's journey as a member of the Seleção squad.

London Calling

For any international soccer player, getting called up to the national team means prestige. It means that you are the kind of player with the caliber to play in a World Cup. For David Luiz, it meant that many of the top teams in Europe would start knocking on Benfica's door, looking for ways to lure David Luiz away from Lisbon and into another European city. After David Luiz's invitation to the Seleção, he was perceived as one of the top defenders.

Rumors started that Real Madrid in Spain would make an offer. Then, there was talk of Arsenal in England. Once the rumor mill gets started, it's hard to tell the difference between fact and fiction. But one fact remained: teams in the European soccer elite wanted David Luiz.

In the end, after all the rumors had died down about where David Luiz might end up for the next season, one team had successfully presented the kind of offer that both Benfica and David Luiz could agree to. That team was Chelsea Football Club, an English club team that is ranked among the top ten most powerful club teams on a global scale. Like Benfica, this was the kind of team that had only one expectation: win.

In January 2011, the boy from Diadema left Lisbon and Benfica for an astounding transfer fee of roughly $31 million, a fee paid directly to the Portuguese club. He was leaving behind friends and fans alike who had been instrumental in his development as an athlete and as a man. After four years with Benfica, it was time for David Luiz to follow a new path. Success had not come overnight for David Luiz, but now he had another exciting opportunity. Only time would tell if he would be able to replicate the same success he had at Benfica as he moved on to London.

In one of his final interviews before leaving for Chelsea, David Luiz said, "I feel a sense of sadness in knowing that I am leaving a place that I invested in, body and soul. This is a club that I have loved and that I will continue to love, but I am also happy that I have the chance to pursue new challenges in my career as a professional soccer player." After David Luiz had accomplished so much with Benfica, it was hard to say good-bye, even though the new place he was going to seemed exciting (since Chelsea is one of the mostly widely recognized soccer clubs in the world).

"If I am ever able to choose the team with which I will retire, Benfica will be my first priority," he said. "Never in my life have I felt this way about a place, a place that made me feel welcome and loved." But amidst Luiz's own mixed feelings about leaving, Chelsea was thrilled to announce that they had secured the services of a Seleção-level defender.

After having coached some of the greatest defenders in the world, including Italian great Paolo Maldini and English giant John Terry, Coach Carlo Ancelotti knew defensive quality when he saw it. So, when Ancelotti started making pre-dictions that David Luiz could someday become the best de-fender in the world, his words were not flippant compliments to a new player. At a time when Chelsea needed to claim their stake in their own

David with Chelsea Manager Carlo Ancelotti during a press conference after David signs with the team.

English national league (known as the Premier League), David Luiz appeared as a possible solution to a club that somehow wasn't winning, despite their impressive cast of characters.

Again, the expectations for the Chelsea team were high. Between Ivorian forward Didier Drogba and Czech goalkeeper Petr Cech, the Chelsea squad was stacked with great players. Once again, David Luiz would have to perform at the very top of his potential, needing to prove that Chelsea's investment in him was worth the money.

New City, New Life

Before moving to London and in only a few years, David Luiz had moved from Diadema to Salvador to Lisbon. Each one of those cities is different from the others in terms of its history and personality. But at least in each one of these cities, David Luiz could understand and speak the language. Even in Lisbon, where the Portuguese is different from the kind spoken in Brazil (imagine the difference between American English and Scottish English, for example), David Luiz could still communicate. If he went to a restaurant and wanted to order a sandwich and a soda, no problem. But now, he was headed to an English-speaking country.

London is one of the great cities of the world. Between Big Ben, Buckingham Palace, and London Bridge, the city is full of landmarks that are known to the world. This is a city of kings and queens, a place so rich with history that it would take years to understand it. Every day London attracts millions of tourists from around the world.

London also plays a special role in the history of soccer as a whole. It was the birthplace of soccer in 1863. London is home to thirteen professional teams, including Arsenal, Fulham, Tottenham Hotspur, and, of course, Chelsea Football Club. Founded in 1905, Chelsea is one of the longest-standing club teams in London. Being a Chelsea fan means joining a fan base full of passion and loyalty. Anyone who has lived in London over the course of the last one hundred years has, in some way, been impacted by the London soccer culture. Daily life and conversation is dominated by talk about how the London teams are doing in their leagues. Now it was David Luiz's turn to experience it.

Soon after moving to the English capital, David Luiz found a home. At the top of a skyscraper that overlooks London Bridge, he found a spacious penthouse apartment. In many ways, this was a sign that he was doing well for himself—that he had arrived and that he was successful. Instead of letting that go to his head, David Luiz took every opportunity to express his gratitude. He even gave jobs to Brazilian immigrants in England, in search of a better life for themselves. He hired Brazilians who were looking for work to help out as cooks and housekeepers in his home.

When Oscar Emboaba, another Brazilian player, joined David Luiz on the Chelsea squad, David Luiz was quick to make Oscar feel welcome and to become a friend. As he himself had gone through adjusting to a new cultural environment, David Luiz could relate to what Oscar was going through.

Emboaba Oscar and David Luiz stretching together during a training session for Chelsea Football Club.

"He knows all about my life, my family," Oscar says. "The kind of friendship we have is also beneficial on the field. David helps me with anything I need." During Oscar's first few months with Chelsea, as he focused more on making sure that he was adjusting well to the style of play than on where he would live, Oscar practically lived at David Luiz's house.

Shining at Stamford Bridge

When David Luiz first arrived in London, Chelsea needed help. Pitted up against the pressure of having to win in order to make their owners (and fans) happy, the Chelsea squad was falling by the wayside in the standings. As the reigning Premier League champions, the pressure was on to repeat as first-place finishers. More than this, the ownership now wanted a title they had never held before: the UEFA Champions League trophy.

Head coach Carlo Ancelotti was determined to get the results the club wanted.

During David Luiz's opening press conference as a new Chelsea player, he stood by Ancelotti's side, smiling from ear to ear, holding his new jersey—the No. 4, which he also wears when he plays on the Seleção for Brazil—as an act of confidence. He was ready to shine for Chelsea, ready to shine on the field of Stamford

Bridge, Chelsea's home stadium in London. He had already been a key part of a European league championship, so who was to say that he couldn't do it again? He would soon find out.

David's opening match for his new team took place on February 6, 2011. He didn't start the game, but he did come onto the field as a replacement for Jose Bosingwa against Liverpool. Even though Chelsea lost this first game of the season, stepping on the field as a member of the Chelsea squad was a dream come true for David.

Only eight days after his first chance to be a part of the action for Chelsea, David Luiz received a Man of the Match award for a Premier League game against Fulham that ended in a scoreless tie. Despite committing a foul in the box, which resulted in a late penalty kick and almost resulted in a loss for his team, his defensive tenacity had already won the hearts of the Chelsea fans. Sometimes, more than being the top skilled player on a team, all a fan wants to see is a player giving their heart and soul for the team, dedicated to every loose ball and defensive play.

Then less than a month after his debut, David Luiz scored his first goal for Chelsea. And this goal didn't come against just any team. Instead, his very first goal for Chelsea came against rival Manchester United, one of the bastions of English soccer. Any time Chelsea and Manchester United play against each other, you see two factions in the stands: one entirely clad in blue, the other in red, each side chanting their team's victory song at the top of their lungs.

In the United States, for instance, every sport has

its major, long-standing rivalries. In baseball, the Yankees – Red Sox matchup is legendary. In the NBA, you've got the Lakers rivaling the Celtics. In England, it is no different. When Chelsea travels to Manchester

David celebrates scoring his first goal as a member of the Chelsea team on March 1, 2011.

to play at United's home stadium, or when Manchester travels to London to play Chelsea, fans and nonfans are on the edge of their seats.

Before the game even began on March 1, 2011, David Luiz knew that he would have a difficult job. Alex Ferguson, Manchester United's legendary coach, had decided to place star forward Wayne Rooney in the front offensive line alongside striker Javier "Chicharito" Hernandez. David Luiz would have to keep an eye on both of these powerhouse players. Either one of them could change the outcome of a game in a single moment.

All throughout the game, playing in the back line as

a sweeper, David Luiz kept his eye on the dangerous attacks of Manchester United and cleared loose balls with enthusiasm and tenacity, trying to prove himself. Every time a ball was crossed in the air, there was David Luiz, his curly hair flailing as he headed away a ball.

In the 29th minute of the game, Wayne Rooney fired a shot past Chelsea goalkeeper Petr Cech, silencing the multitude of Chelsea fans. The first half ended 1−0 in favor of Manchester United. Now, Chelsea had only forty-five minutes to reverse the tide to give their home crowd a victory at Stamford Bridge.

When both teams returned from the locker room for the start of the second half, Chelsea wouldn't take long to begin their comeback. Chelsea midfielder Michael Essien crossed the ball into the box. The ball was knocked around until it landed to the right side of the penalty box, where David Luiz was in the right place at the right time.

The ball took one bounce. David Luiz wound up a powerful kick. And the rest is history. He volleyed in a shot past veteran United goalkeeper Edwin Van Der Sar and put Chelsea on the scoreboard. With ten minutes left in the game, Chelsea captain Frank Lampard would score the winning goal after a penalty kick was called in the box. Final score: Chelsea 2−1, and David Luiz had shone as a newcomer to the Manchester−Chelsea rivalry.

In June 2011, looking back at his first few months in London, David Luiz said, "I arrived to Chelsea, and thanks to God, I was able to play straight away and show what I could give to the team."

Home and Away

As a professional soccer player, David Luiz spends most of his time on the road. Countless road trips, along with a tiresome match schedule, are a regular part of his life, regardless of where in the world he is. After all, from one day to the next he might be playing in a different city or country or continent. Beyond the high-dollar contracts lies a desire to simply feel at home. Fortunately for David Luiz, he has learned how to establish roots whenever soccer takes him somewhere new.

In Lisbon, the local fans utterly adored David Luiz as a Benfica player because he made a point to connect with the people of Lisbon. At the height of his success in Portugal, he once said, "I've learned to love Benfica, to live Benfica. I've learned that just stepping onto the field and playing is not enough. Being a player here needs to be so much more than that. I need to understand how people feel, how the kids watching us feel, how the elderly ladies who root for us feel. That gives me the chills. I do everything I can to return the kindness that our fans give us. No amount of money can replace that feeling."

Even as a Chelsea player living and playing in London, David Luiz remembers those who have supported him throughout his career. On December 20, 2013, for instance, David Luiz made a special trip to Lisbon in order to support a little girl named Leonor who was battling cancer. He was part of a three-hour televised benefit event in honor of Leonor and other children with cancer all over Portugal. If there is a need that David Luiz can help with, he will be there, no strings attached. These kinds of decisions endear him to his fans all over the world.

For David Luiz, the fans are the people who make the game worth playing. So at Chelsea, David Luiz considers himself a "Geezer," a term for die-hard Chelsea fans. On his Twitter and Instagram, he often refers to the fact that he is just one more "Geezer," no more special than any kid or adult in London watching the Chelsea squad play on TV. In other words, David Luiz is loyal to the people wherever he is living and playing at the time, and he remains loyal to them.

His personality is the kind that draws people in, making them feel important—the kind of person that makes others feel valued. Fellow Seleção player Dani Alves says, "David Luiz is not just a friend, he has a lot of quality too."

These are the values he was raised with in Diadema.

When asked about his childhood there, David Luiz says, "I come from a family with a lot of needs, but my parents were blessed by always having enough to cover our basic needs.... As someone who had to leave home at a very young age, I learned that I had to give up certain things if I ever wanted to get somewhere in life." Even as someone who now looks at the possibility of playing in a World Cup as an almost sure thing, he has never forgotten his roots.

Even as he shined at Benfica and wasn't getting called up to the Seleção, he never thought of abandoning the hope that someday he would have the chance to wear the yellow jersey of his home country. When asked about the possibility of becoming a Portuguese citizen and instead playing for Portugal's national team, David Luiz simply replied, "Playing for the Seleção is a dream I've had since I was a kid, and it's always been my family's dream for me. I would only truly experience playing in the World Cup for my country. Otherwise, it would just be another team to me." Whenever he gets a chance, David Luiz returns to Brazil to see old friends and family. During one such visit, he came home to a house decorated with pictures of his greatest accomplishments in soccer. His parents still saw him as the young kid who had left home to chase a dream, to run after God's plan for his life wherever it would take him.

Awards Given to David Luiz

Portuguese League Player of the Year
(2009 - 2010)

Man of the Match Award
(February 2011)

Premier League Player of the Month
(March 2011)

Professional Footballers' Association
Fans Player of the Month
(March 2011)

FIFA World Club Cup Silver Boot Award
(December 2012)

Champion of Champions

Today, there are two soccer tournaments that capture the world's attention. One, of course, is the World Cup, held every four years as the epitome of what soccer can do to bring the world together. The other is the UEFA Champions League, where the best teams in Europe compete. Every time a Champions League match is played, an epic battle takes place on the field. Picture one of the battles in *The Lord of the Rings* or one of your favorite comic book hero movies and you'll start to understand a little more about the intensity that comes in the Champions League.

When David Luiz arrived in Chelsea in 2011, Chelsea was hungry for a title. They had never won the top prize in the Champions League. David had already played matches in the Champions League for Benfica. But this time, something was different for him. For Benfica, he was just a kid trying to make the starting team. Eventually, of course, his efforts paid off. On Chelsea, however, he was playing to uphold a reputation.

Thus, at the start of the 2011–2012 season, David Luiz was well aware of the pressures that came with playing in this context, on this stage. And, just as he had learned to do through hard work in practice, determination on game day, and faith in his life overall, he would not disappoint.

Along the way, Chelsea would have to face all kinds of challenges, both off and on the field. But then, sometimes the best stories are those in which someone overcomes a great challenge. Picture yourself climbing a mountain with a group of people. Now, picture yourself racing to the top of the mountain against twenty other teams of people. If this seems like an impossible task, then just imagine the difficulty involved in winning the UEFA Champions League. This is what David Luiz and the rest of the Chelsea team were up against. These were some of the most important games along the way that David Luiz faced with his new teammates.

Chelsea 2, Bayer Leverkusen 0:

This was the first time that David Luiz started with the team. He took the spot of captain John Terry in the defensive back line, a big honor for a relative newcomer to the club. John Terry was allowed to sit out for a one-game breather, and David Luiz made the most of the opportunity. His big moment came in the 67th minute when he scored a goal for his team after a brilliant

Chelsea performance in the second half. In the final seconds of the game, Chelsea midfielder Juan Mata put closing numbers to the match.

Chelsea 3, Valencia 0:

Sometimes in soccer, even the most tense games turn out to be less daunting than expected. So when Chelsea played Spanish club Valencia in the group stages, within three minutes striker Didier Drogba's goal put the minds of Chelsea's fans to rest. Even though Valencia then dominated possession on the field, they could not score. What's more, Ramires scored a second goal for Chelsea midway through the first half. Then Drogba made it three in the 76th minute. Thus, Chelsea stamped their passport for the next round, the play-offs, of the Champions League.

Chelsea 5, Napoli 4 (on aggregate): First Play-off Matchup

The way it works in the Champions League is that you play one home game and one away game against each team. In the end, the overall (called the aggregate) score determines which team will advance to the next round.

The first game, played in Naples, Italy, ended in disaster for Chelsea. The Londoners lost 3–1. Only a miracle could change things. The second game ended 4–1 in Chelsea's favor. They inched ahead of Napoli by one goal, which guaranteed them a spot in the next round of the Champions League play-offs.

Chelsea 3, Benfica 1 (on aggregate): Quarterfinals

David Luiz was now forced to play against the team he had grown to love, the team that had projected him onto the world stage. Chelsea was scheduled to play Benfica in the quarterfinals of the Champions League. Needless to say, David's emotions were mixed.

In the end, however, Chelsea prevailed over the Portuguese side, winning 3–1 on aggregate.

Then right before the most important matchup of his career up to that point—a semifinal in the Champions League against Barcelona—David Luiz got injured. In a Premier League match against Tottenham, David Luiz was carried off the field with a pulled hamstring. As the clash with Barcelona neared, Chelsea fans could only hope that David Luiz's absence wouldn't be a determining factor.

Chelsea 3, Barcelona 2 (on aggregate): Semifinals

David Luiz was out of the picture against Barcelona. And nobody believed that Chelsea could knock out defending Champions League titleholders Barcelona in the semifinals. But then again . . . Chelsea survived their two games against Barcelona, winning the first game 1–0 then coming from behind in the second game to tie 2–2.

Chelsea 1, Bayern 1 (5 – 4 on Penalty Kicks): Final

For the final game of the Champions League, the championship game, David Luiz was cleared from his injury. At the time, Bayern was considered an amazing team, with an unstoppable goal scoring force driving its offense.

After Bayern Munich (German team) scored toward the latter part of the second half, many people believed that game was over, that Chelsea's good play had suddenly come to an end. But only a few minutes later, Didier Drogba scored a goal.

When regulation time ended, Chelsea and Bayern were forced into a penalty kick shootout. Chelsea's kickers all delivered. Each one of them scored a shot. Chelsea was finally the champion of the most important soccer tournament on the planet. David's first year with Chelsea was the year Chelsea finally won the UEFA Champions League title.

David Luiz's Soccer Career

São Paulo youth squad (1999 – 2001)

The Brazilian team holds the most national league titles — six in all. They have won the FIFA World Club Championship three times, as well as the South American version of the UEFA Champions League — the Libertadores Cup — three times.

Vitória (2001 – 2007, youth and professional squad)

Alongside E. C. Bahia, this is the biggest club team from the Brazilian state of Bahia. They have struggled with relegation in the past, but are currently stable in the Série A.

Benfica (2007 – 2011)

This team from the capital city of Lisbon and often Portugal's most serious contender in international tournaments has proven itself to be the most successful team in Portuguese League history.

Chelsea (2011 – present)

One of the most widely recognized soccer brands in the world and one of the most successful teams in the history of the English Premier League, Chelsea is the most recent English winner of the highly coveted UEFA Champions League title, which they won in 2012.

On and Off the Field

David Luiz is known as someone who is always smiling. And his joy is contagious on and off the field. His big, fluffy, curly hair is a perfect match to his personality. On both Benfica and Chelsea, he has sometimes played funny pranks on his teammates. Back at Benfica, David Luiz would sometimes grab a video camera to capture his teammates' postgame reactions. For an international soccer superstar, he's the kind of guy you just might want to have as a friend. But for all his goofiness and good humor, he also embraces his responsibilities as a role model.

As David Luiz played for Chelsea, he understood the importance of each and every minute of the matches he played in. He was carving a place for himself in the history of the Chelsea Football Club. On October 19, 2011, David Luiz would create a different kind of moment.

In order to fully understand this moment, though, you need to understand a little more about one of David Luiz's teammates, Fernando Torres. Labeled by many as one of the deadliest strikers in the world of football, Fernando Torres was facing criticism because many people feel that he was not playing as well as he could be. For any athlete, this is heartbreaking. The year 2010 marked the year of Torres's strange decline, and many were wondering what had happened to the player who had shown so much promise in other years, in other seasons.

Even at a very young age, Torres earned the nickname El Nino (The Kid), because he started dazzling his coaches as a child and never stopped doing so. He began his career with one of Spain's most respected teams, Atletico Madrid, where in 2001 he became the youngest player to ever play for the squad. At the age of nineteen, he earned the captain's armband, another record in terms of age. For six years, Torres was loyal to the Atletico family, scoring goals and showing remarkable hustle on the field. In the summer of 2007, a multi-million-dollar deal from Liverpool lured Torres into the prestige of the Premier League.

In his first season, Torres scored thirty-three goals—more than the tally set by Dutch legend Ruud van Nistelrooy, a former Manchester United player—and became the highest-scoring foreign rookie in English soccer. While he kept up this high level of play with Liverpool, he also began to struggle with injuries. In 2010, Torres played in the World Cup with his home country, Spain, and lifted the World Cup championship trophy with his teammates. But he got injured in the final game against the Netherlands.

Despite El Nino's great success on the world stage, when he joined the Chelsea Football Club, Torres was struggling. He was a goal-scorer that simply wasn't scoring goals. He had been hired to give Chelsea wins. And he was struggling to get the fans at Stamford Bridge to truly believe in him. But one teammate stepped up and showed his support—the boy from Diadema.

On this particular occasion in 2011, the opponent facing off against Chelsea was Racing Genk, a Belgian club. Nobody expected this team to go very far in the tournament, but still, this was the Champions League, where anything could happen.

Knowing that Torres was desperate to score goals for Chelsea, David Luiz approached his teammate. The television cameras from the game show David Luiz, clad in the traditional Chelsea blue, walking over to Fernando Torres and praying for him. Rather than giving him hints about the opponents' defense or lightening the mood with a prematch joke, David Luiz chose to step out in faith and prayed for his teammate. As David Luiz placed one hand on Torres's shoulder and the other hand on Torres's head, his lips uttered something up to heaven. David Luiz's closed eyes seemed to prompt Torres to close his own eyes. This was a clear image of hope, of unity, of faith.

Then the game started. After hitting the post in his first shot on goal, Torres then went on to score two goals, leading the way to a 5–0 victory for the boys in blue. In Champions League, this kind of score is rare because

the best teams are all competing with one another. In the highlight reel of the match against Genk, there is a look of joy on El Nino's face, mixed in with the relief that came from returning to his natural habitat as a striker. But the win wasn't the only memorable moment.

David Luiz has made a ritual of praying for teammate Torres before games.

Rather than just talking about his faith in God, David Luiz was ready to put it into action by praying for a teammate. While soccer is in the end only a game, it's also so much more than that. It's an opportunity to show the world what you're made of and how you act when the cameras are on, when the pressure is mounting all around you, when thousands of fans place their trust in you to play hard on their behalf. Once again, David Luiz had made a powerful statement to the world about the kind of person he was.

One Year from the World Cup

After two seasons with Chelsea, it was time for David Luiz to take part in the Confederations Cup in Brazil as a key member of the Seleção. Remember that the entire nation was consumed by protests that were happening all around the country. The Brazilian fans had mixed emotions. Some thought that this tournament was coming at a bad time for Brazil, that too many frustrations were building up in the Brazilian people in order for people to really enjoy the tournament. Others were thrilled about the chance for the Seleção team to prove itself, to tell the world that Brazilian soccer was in fact still the best in the world. Regardless of anyone's opinion, the tournament was going to happen, and since Brazil was the host country for the World Cup, they were also the host country for the Confederations Cup in 2013.

Game One: Brazil vs. Japan

To the delight of the Brazilian soccer fans, Brazil started their Confederations Cup campaign with a stunning win.

Before the game began, though, Brazilian president Dilma Rousseff officially announced the competition. As she spoke, many of the Brazilian fans in the stadium booed. So the president of FIFA got up and asked the fans where their "fair play," or sportsmanship, was.

But once the Seleção took to the field, the home crowd of more than 67,000 fans at the Mané Garrincha National Stadium in the capital city of Brasilia cheered from the opening whistle to the final moments. The stadium was contagious with Brazil Fever. With goals from Neymar, a beautiful volley kick in the opening minutes of the match, midfielder Paulinho, and striker Jô, in the closing seconds of the match, Brazil ended up winning the game with a commanding 3–0 final score.

Game Two: Brazil vs. Mexico

At the gorgeous Castelao Arena in the beautiful city of Fortaleza, Brazil won its second consecutive game of the tournament. In the 9th minute of the game, Neymar slid a left-footed kick past Mexican goalkeeper Corona. Later, to finish the game, Neymar created a play in the middle of two Mexican defenders and passed the ball to Jo, who simply had to tap the ball into the back of the net.

Game Three: Brazil vs. Italy

This game took David back to the city of Salvador, where he had spent so much time at Vitória, years earlier.

Neymar would score his third goal in his third straight game. Fred, with two goals, and defender Dante would finish up the tally for the Seleção, with a final score of 4–2.

On the outside of the soccer stadiums, however, protests continued. David Luiz, through his personal Facebook and Instagram pages, saw a need to connect with people. He reminded Brazilians that on the field, each player was just a dreamer, a man who was once a boy playing somewhere in Brazil and hoping to someday wear the Seleção jersey.

Game Four: Brazil vs. Uruguay

In the renovated Mineirao stadium, to tens of thousands of expectant Brazilian fans, Brazil would face Uruguay, its complicated South American rival who reminded so many of the World Cup final loss in 1950. From the moment the match started, it was clear that this was going to be a thrilling game.

David Luiz was trying to guard Uruguayan captain Diego Lugano in the box, and the referee called a penalty kick after both players used their arms to try to get an advantage on the play. The boy from Diadema most certainly would not want to be remembered as the player who allowed a strong opponent to move ahead on the scoreboard. Uruguayan forward Diego Forlan got the ball, went to the line, and got ready to take the kick. Meanwhile, Brazil's goalkeeper, Julio Cesar, prepared to try and stop the kick. The whistle blew, and the entire stadium held their breath.

But when Forlan kicked the ball, the moment became a Brazilian celebration. Julio Cesar had saved the kick, sending the Mineirao into a frenzy. David Luiz could breathe a little more easily now, knowing that his foul wasn't going to cost his team the game. Minutes later, Fred would score for Brazil. While Uruguay would tie the game later, eventually Paulinho would put final touches in the game, with a late header. The Mineirao was on fire, ablaze with national pride.

The Seleção was on to the final match. Their opponent: Spain, the reigning champions of the world. And the boy from Diadema would have a chance to be a part of history.

Confederations Cup Final: Brazil vs. Spain

The final game of the stadium was to be held at the legendary Maracanã Stadium, in the heart of Rio de Janeiro. Tens of thousands of Brazilian soccer fanatics filled the stadium. David Luiz, sporting his No. 4 Seleção jersey, waited for an opportunity to make history with the Brazilian national team.

Before the game began, the Brazilian anthem stopped playing before it had ended, which prompted the entire stadium to keep singing in its loudest voice to the very end of the song. This was a display of unity, set against the backdrop of protests that called for change in the country of soccer. A mere ninety-six seconds into the game, Hulk crossed the ball in from the right side of the field, and Fred, the striker who was making a name for himself as a natural-born goal scorer, put the ball in the back of the net.

Ten minutes later, in what could be considered the greatest play for him so far, David Luiz saved his team. Spanish player Pedro, a very skilled forward, had already beaten Brazilian goalkeeper Julio Cesar on the play and simply had to tap the ball into the back of the net.

David makes the best save of his career during the FIFA Confederations Cup Brazil 2013 Final match between Brazil and Spain.

The shot went off, and the fans at the Maracanã knew for certain that Pedro's ball would go in. But they had forgotten about David Luiz. They weren't aware of the countless hours David Luiz had spent preparing for a defining soccer moment. As the ball went past the goalie, the Chelsea defender from Diadema slid in and cleared it off the line. Immediate replays showed that the ball was clearly headed to the back of the net. David Luiz had rescued his team.

Later, in the 44th minute, Neymar made it 2–0. Three minutes later, Fred would put the finishing touches on the game, as Brazil would win the tournament. The win boosted the spirits of the Brazilian fans; now they couldn't wait for the World Cup.

True Colors

Some coaches use positive messages and encouraging words to motivate their players: "Good hustle!" or "Great idea!" Then there are coaches who are known for their stoic, tight-lipped, "frowny" style, who are rarely impressed by their players, even when their players do the impossible. Portuguese-born Jose Mourinho is one such coach.

After a lackluster 2013 season at the helm of the Chelsea squad, the coach for Chelsea was fired. So the team owners chose Jose Mourinho as the new coach. Coach Mourinho had coached Real Madrid in Spain for three seasons and was looking for a new set of challenges. Many fans were excited about his return to Chelsea Football Club because Coach Mourinho had led the team to Premier League glory in the past.

After the euphoria of winning the Confederations

Cup, the members of the Brazilian squad were ready and eager to prove that their victory had not been a home crowd fluke. So David was coming off a dazzling performance in the Confederations Cup final and heading back to Chelsea to work under the new tough-minded coach.

But even after having proved himself so many times, from earning a starting spot on the Benfica starting eleven to winning the UEFA Champions League with Chelsea in a thrilling championship match, David would once again have to earn his stripes with a new coach with a unique style of leadership.

While David kept a humble posture in this period of transition for Chelsea, he had grown used to starting every game. That wasn't the case this season. In the "Mourinho style" of play, there was no longer a guaranteed spot for David Luiz in the starting eleven.

Chelsea's head coach, Jose Mourinho, talks to David after he was fouled during a game.

With one of the top defensive rosters in the world, Mourinho was not going to keep players in the starting lineup just because they had been brilliant in the past. So David would need to keep working hard to prove himself.

Even when Coach Mourinho benched David Luiz, he decided to keep a positive attitude, acknowledging once more that God was in charge of his future. There was no need to worry about how much or how little he would play if he was trying his best, which was something David had grown accustomed to doing. "I know that God knows everything in my life, so, when I don't play, sometimes I consult with Him," explained Luiz.

Building Excitement

To say that David Luiz is excited for the 2014 World Cup would be an understatement. As a dreaming kid in Diadema, only in his wildest dreams would he be a part of the Seleção, playing a World Cup on the soil of his home country. And for David, the Seleção is more than just a team; it's a family. After winning the Confederations Cup, he described the team by saying, "It's the best atmosphere I've had in my life as a team—the friendship . . . all of us on the team thinking the same way."

What makes the tournament all the more special for David is the fact that the opening match of the Cup will be played in São Paulo, not far from where he grew up. The brand-new Arena de São Paulo, or Arena Corinthians, will serve as the opening stage for one of the biggest matches of David's career.

So on December 6, 2013, David's mind was on one

thing only, the group drawing for the 2014 FIFA World Cup. Every time the World Cup rolls around, several months before the tournament, the host country organizes an event in which each one of the thirty-two teams is given a specific group to play in. Each team faces off against every other team in their respective groups, and the top two teams in each group advance to the play-off round.

For this particular event, the Brazilian organizers decided to hold the group drawing in Costa do Sauipe, a tropical Brazilian paradise. After the last team

Oscar (L), Hulk (C) and David Luiz during a training session for the Seleção.

had been selected, the final groups of the tournament had been decided. Now, part of the mystery was gone. Every national team squad knew the three first teams that they would have to face in order to advance to the next round of the world's biggest soccer festival. Brazil was in Group A:

Group A

Brazil

Cameroon

Croatia

Mexico

This would undoubtedly be a challenging group, even though Brazil was highly favored to take first place.

Brazil had struggled against Mexico. Cameroon, led by star striker Samuel Eto'o, and Croatia, led by the skill of midfielder Modric, would all be competing at high levels.

The Seleção now had the ability to scout their known matchups, scouring for information about their opponents' strengths and weaknesses. Strategies, tendencies, game plans—anything and everything that would give the team an indication of how they could best confront their opponents on the soccer field. Excitement was rising with every moment, as now every day ticked down to the start of the tournament, when all of the world's eyes would be glued to Brazil. With thirteen cities scattered around the nation, each and every arena a representation of all the hard work and dedication put into hosting the event, every location was key.

In December 2013, Nike, the sponsoring company of the Seleção, put together an ad campaign called "Ouse Ser Brasileiro," which literally means "Dare to Be Brazilian." In a country experiencing so much unrest and disagreement, the feeling of national pride had to be rescued, even if a bunch of soccer players were now responsible for carrying it out. Nike chose Neymar, Thiago Silva, Paulinho, David Luiz, and Bernard as the players to be the face of the campaign.

In David Luiz's segment, the sheriff of the Seleção defensive line, David Luiz turns into a giant, fierce, animated version of himself and defends by helping his team clear the ball away. The ad closes with the words, "No one plays like us," a statement that could very well be a summary of the last eighty years of Brazilian soccer history.

Within the first few days of the video being released, tens of thousands of Brazilians had watched it. Here was a reminder of Brazil's great history in the sport, a reminder that the country had produced some of the best players in the history of the game. And David Luiz, the boy from Diadema, the kid who moved away from home to pursue his soccer dreams when he was just a teenager, was being touted as one of the great hopes for success at the World Cup.

Host Cities of the World Cup 2014 in Brazil

- Belo Horizonte
- Brasilia
- Cuiabá
- Curitiba
- Fortaleza
- Manaus
- Natal
- Porto Alegre
- Recife
- Rio de Janeiro
- Salvador
- São Paulo

More Than a Game

Imagine for a second that you've been asked to go somewhere that only the most talented, intelligent, gifted people are able to go. Maybe that place is the White House, where so many leaders have made extremely important decisions. Maybe that place is Yankee Stadium, a place that carries on the legacy of some of the greatest baseball players to ever walk the earth.

Now imagine a small school in a poor neighborhood, its teachers and students struggling with their basic needs. Imagine seeing a kindergarten student, shivering in the cold due to a lack of a warm jacket. In your mind, where would you rather be?

David Luiz is in both places. Even though he is an international soccer star, David still cares about the people in his nation, especially people like his own family and neighbors. Because he sees his life as filled with

More Than a Game

Darren Walsh/Chelsea via AP Images

Chelsea's Oscar and David Luiz play table football with young fans during a fundraising event in January 2013. David seeks to show that everything he has comes from the fact that he has a great responsibility to help others in need.

blessings, he believes he has a great responsibility to help others in need. He founded and funds a charity called Acao Social David Luiz (David Luiz Social Action), an organization that provides food and special events.

There are people in Brazil, people who had grown up in towns just like Diadema and who could very easily have been his neighbors, who were struggling to make ends meet. Imagine a community struggling with poverty, kids with only one pair of shoes or a handful of outfits, receiving a visit from an organization sponsored by one of the country's most beloved soccer players. Thanks to the work of the David Luiz Social Action project, this kind of scene is taking place all over the country of

93

Brazil, bringing canned food to families who need it and hosting fun events for underprivileged children.

In August 2013, Regina Célia, David's mother, visited a small school in the small town of Cataguases, a town of hardworking people of modest means, on behalf of the David Luiz Social Action project. She helped give brand-new soccer balls, David Luiz T-shirts, and nutritious snacks to nearly one hundred kids. In fact, Regina does a lot of the work for the organization, acting as an ambassador for the values that David stands for.

This can be the beauty of soccer. On the one hand, it's just a game. Eleven players versus another eleven on the other side battling to score more goals than the other team. But David and his family know what soccer can really do for others. Although David Luiz has been able to provide for his family financially, he doesn't see his success as something that he's entitled to, or something that he has somehow deserved more than anyone else. He knows where the credit is due: "Everything in life belongs to God."

Barcelona

When you talk about soccer today, there is one name that you cannot leave out: Lionel Messi. Quite simply, Messi is the greatest player of his generation. From 2009 to 2012, Lionel Messi received the honor of FIFA World Player of the Year, setting a record by winning the prize four consecutive times. Messi is a goal-scoring machine, an unstoppable force for his club team, Barcelona, and his track record only supports the praise that soccer fans all over the world have given him. While David Luiz has played with some of the greatest names in soccer himself, the potential of one day playing alongside Messi would be exciting to any player. And, just maybe, that possibility would come true for David.

If you follow international soccer, the word Barcelona has a special ring to it. For millions of fans around the world, the name represents a team adored by so many, a team that so often delights its fans with the best soccer in the world. To others, Barcelona is one of the most feared adversaries in the history of the sport and recruits talent from all over the world. Like the New York Yankees or the Dallas Cowboys, most people either love them or hate them.

What is certain is that Barcelona attracts only elite players, the cream of the crop. And as Barcelona prepares for another quest to win not only its national league but also the UEFA Champions League, they came knocking at Chelsea's door, looking for a player to add tenacity and skill to their defensive back line. They want the boy from Diadema, David Luiz.

Without a doubt, Barcelona is the king of Spanish soccer. The team has won eighty-three national championship titles. Considered by many soccer experts to be the greatest club team of all time, Barcelona is also one of the most supported teams in the world. In Spain, the whole country stops to behold "El Clasico," the term given to any game played against Barcelona's rival Real Madrid.

Ten Barcelona players have won the FIFA World Player of the Year Award. In 2010 Barcelona made history by having three of its players place as the top three players in the world. In the four years that former Spanish national and Barcelona player Pep Guardiola coached the team, many considered the Barcelona squad, with Messi at the helm, to be the greatest team of all time.

The invitation to play for Barcelona is not simple, though. David is still under contract with Chelsea. The

London team would have to agree to release David for a fee. Despite the fact that Coach Mourinho has benched David, the coach still publicly declares that Chelsea has every intention of holding on to him. In an interview with Express, Mourinho even said that David Luiz "has what it takes to be the best defender in the world." As a key member of the Seleção and less than a year from the start of the 2014 World Cup, David is now in an interesting situation.

On the one hand, at Chelsea, David has an opportunity to persevere under a coach who has a high standard for excellence. And David has only been on the Chelsea team for two and a half seasons. Besides, David has made a home in London among the tens of thousands of Chelsea fans who want him to remain on the Chelsea

David Luiz, the "sheriff" of the backline, makes a defensive header.

squad. On the other hand, no professional soccer player can ever take an invitation from Barcelona lightly. In Barcelona, he would have the chance to play alongside the world's greatest player, Lionel Messi, along with the rising star and Seleção teammate, Neymar.

As 2013 drew to a close, the rumors that David Luiz would transfer to Barcelona in the next transfer window only got stronger. Considered to be a valuable asset to any team in the world, and sitting the bench at Chelsea, all signs pointed to a move from England to Spain.

All throughout his career, he has time and again stated that his life belongs to God. Maybe it doesn't matter where he plays as much as it matters how he plays. And at this point, he has become the kind of player who is known for hard work, perseverance, and faith. None of that would change if he moved teams. For the next few months, no matter where his professional soccer career lands him, he is still wearing the No. 4 jersey for his home country in the most important soccer championship of the world.

Bibliography

"Adaptado no Chelsea, Oscar se acostuma com a vida em Londres com video game e 'aulas' de David Luiz." ESPN Brasil. Nov. 11, 2012. http://www.youtube.com/watch?v=hLta5Tyac0k.

"Almost half the world tuned in at home to watch 2010 FIFA World Cup South Africa." FIFA.com. July 11, 2011. http://www.fifa.com/worldcup/archive/south africa2010/organisation/media/newsid=1473143/.

Canônico, Leandro and Márcio Iannacca. "Brasilidades: David Luiz, rei das pipas em Diadema, busca o céu de Londres." Globo Esporte. May 31, 2013. http://globoesporte.globo.com/futebol/selecao-brasileira/noticia/2013/05/brasilidades-david-luiz-rei-das-pipas-em-diadema-quer-ceu-de-londres.html.

"Chelsea 1–0 Barcelona—Roberto DiMatteo on David Luiz (4/18/2012)." YouTube. April 18, 2012. http://www.youtube.com/watch?v=KX7E9em2GDg.

"Chelsea FC—End of Season Interview: David Luiz." Chelsea Football Club, June 6, 2011. http://www.youtube.com/watch?v=AkKKAQA7_CA.

"Cidades-Sede." Portal 2014. http://www.portal2014.org.br/cidades-sedes/.

"Copa das Confederações." Globo Esporte. http://globoesporte.globo.com/futebol/copa-das-confederacoes/.

"David Luiz Fala Sobre Benfica e Carreira." Fãs d'Esportes. Jan. 4, 2011. http://www.youtube.com/watch?v=t84W4Yj6–3U.

"David Luiz Fala Sobre Mano Menezes e Seleção." Fãs d'Esportes. Jan. 5, 2011. http://www.youtube.com/watch?v=FAeKMkJ76as.

"David Luiz Mostra Sua Casa ao Fãs d'Esportes." Fãs d'Esportes. Jan. 6, 2011. http://www.youtube.com/watch?v=TvYz-o9HGzI.

"David Luiz no Programa SLB (parte 1)." YouTube. July 13, 2010. http://www.youtube.com/watch?v=mM9jH4UbCk0.

"David Luiz no Programa SLB (parte 2)." YouTube. July 13, 2010. http://www.youtube.com/watch?v=m6KDlj6PhII.

"David Luiz set to complete Chelsea transfer." A Football Report. Jan. 23, 2011. http://transfers.afootballreport.com/post/2894205083/david-luiz-set-to-complete-chelsea-transfer.

"David Luiz Shows His Apartment." Ao Vivo. Jan. 13, 2013. http://www.youtube.com/watch?v=mdNrDQrJwf4.

"David Luiz: Levo o Benfica no Coração." YouTube. Feb. 1, 2011. http://www.youtube.com/watch?v=H2V9_m7Hjzc.

"Fernando Torres—Player Bio." ESPNFC.com. http://espnfc.com/player/_/id/24257/fernando-torres?cc=5901.

Gazeta Press. "Ex-técnicos destacam a ascensão de David Luiz." Placar. Feb. 2, 2011. http://placar.abril.com.br/materia/ex-tecnicos-destacam-a-ascensao-de-david-luiz.

Hayes, Garry. "The Cult of David Luiz: Why the Chelsea and Brazil Star Is so Loved." Bleacher Report. Dec. 19, 2013. http://bleacherreport.com/articles/1887111-the-cult-of-david-luiz-why-the-chelsea-and-brazil-star-is-so-loved.

Hayward, Joshua. "Transfer Rumour Rater: David Luiz to Barcelona in the January Transfer Window." Bleacher Report. Dec. 3, 2013. http://bleacherreport.com/articles/1874365-transfer-rumour-rater-david-luiz-to-barcelona-in-the-january-transfer-window.

Henriques, Inês, Bruno Miguel Dias. "Benfica é campeão." Sapo Desporto. May 9, 2010. http://desporto.sapo.pt/futebol/primeira_liga/artigo/2010/05/09/benfica_campe_o.html.

Jenson, Pete. "Luiz's Christian faith behind Chelsea's hands-on attitude." The Independent. Oct. 21, 2011. http://www.independent.co.uk/sport/football/european/luizs-christian-faith-behind-chelseas-handson-attitude-2373581.html.

Krishnan, Joe. "David Luiz: How the Chelsea Defender Became One of the Best in Europe." Bleacher Report. May 23, 2013. http://bleacherreport.com/articles/1649593-david-luiz-how-the-chelsea-defender-became-one-of-the-best-in-europe.

"Lionel Messi Biography." Messi.com. http://www.messi
.com/.

Lopes, Artur Louback "Como se Tornar um Jogador de
Futebol?" Mundo Estranho. Dec. 2013. http://mundo
estranho.abril.com.br/materia/como-se-tornar-
um-jogador-de-futebol.

"Luiz Fulfills Promise to Parents." FIFA.com. Feb.
12, 2011. http://www.fifa.com/world-match-centre/
nationalleagues/nationalleague=england-premier-
league – 2000000000/news/newsid/138/153/9/
index.html.

Lustig, Nick. "Dani Alves wants friend David Luiz to
leave Chelsea and join him at Barcelona." The Daily
Star. Aug. 12, 2013. http://www.dailystar.co.uk/
sport/football/332060/Dani-Alves-wants-friend-
David-Luiz-to-leave-Chelsea-and-join-him-at-
Barcelona.

"The Magician of Maracanazo." FIFA.com. http://www
.fifa.com/classicfootball/players/player=174559/.

McNulty, Phil. "Chelsea 2 – 1 Manchester United."
BBCSport. March 1, 2011. http://news.bbc.co.uk/
sport2/hi/football/eng_prem/9405635.stm.

Morlidge, Matthew. "David Luiz Exclusive: You English
don't believe—but you need to dream. Go to Brazil
and expect to win the World Cup!" Daily Mail. Dec.
4, 2013. http://www.dailymail.co.uk/sport/world
cup2014/article – 2517972/David-Luiz-English-dont-
believe-win-World-Cup.html.

"Nike—Ouse ser brasileiro (Ninguem joga como a gente)." Nikefutebol. Dec. 1, 2013, http://www.youtube.com/watch?v=-HlBqson5dg.

"Ola, sou o David Luiz—entrevista," YouTube, Feb. 26, 2011, http://www.youtube.com/watch?v=lE4cSsv Tdjs.

"Origens: paixão pela bola e amor ao Brasil levam David Luiz à Seleção," Globo Esporte, April 21, 2013, http://globoesporte.globo.com/programas/esporte-espetac ular/noticia/2013/04/origens-aposta-do-brasil-david-luiz-quase-defendeu-selecao-de-portugal.html.

Redação PLACAR, "David Luiz posta foto no vestiário e exalta a nova família Scolari," Placar, Oct. 15, 2013, http://placar.abril.com.br/materia/david-luiz-posta-foto-no-vestiario-e-exalta-a-nova-familia-scolari.

Redação. "Brasil: David Luiz convocado por Mano Menezes." Mais Futebol. July 27, 2010. http://www.maisfutebol.iol.pt/benfica-brasil-internacio nal-david-luiz-maisfutebol-futebol-iol/520b8 7703004bc615fd26605.html.

Regio, Anderson, André Naddeo, and Diego Garcia. "David Luiz chora e diz: 'trocaria tudo pelo título mundial." Terra. Dec. 16, 2012. http://esportes.terra.com.br/futebol/mundialdeclubes/david-luiz-chora-e-diz-trocaria-tudo-pelo-titulo-mundial,648e1166524ab 310VgnVCM4000009bcceb0aRCRD.html.

Rocha, Felipe. "Baixinho para o São Paulo, David Luiz desponta na seleção de Mano." IG Esporte. Nov. 15,

2010. http://esporte.ig.com.br/futebol/2010/11/15/
baixinho+para+o+sao+paulo+david+luiz+desponta
+na+selecao+de+mano+10131141.html.

Rozeno, Marcos. "David Luiz, um cristão mais que vence-
dor." O Melhor Do Gospel. http://www.omelhordo
gospel.com/default.asp?pagina=noticia&txtcod
igo=1192.

Skara, Kristian, Frank Roger Vangen and Joakim
Melseth. "World Cup History." worldcup-history.com.
http://www.worldcup-history.com/index.php?
width=1280.

Sportsmail Reporter. "Luiz's 'healing hands' are no gim-
mick: Brazilian's faith runs deeper than helping Torres."
Daily Mail. Oct. 21, 2011. http://www.dailymail
.co.uk/sport/football/article−2051837/David-Luizs-
healing-hands-gimmick.html.

"UEFA Champions League—David Luiz." UEFA.com.
June 5, 2013. http://www.uefa.com/uefachampions-
league/season=2014/clubs/player=1900733/profile/
index.html.

"UEFA Champions League 2011/12." UEFA.com. May
28, 2012. http://www.uefa.com/uefachampionsleague
/season=2012/clubs/club=52914/matches/index
.html.

"USA Falls to Brazil 2−0 in Front of 77,223 Fans at the
New Meadowlands Stadium." US Soccer. Aug. 10, 2010.
http://www.ussoccer.com/news/mens-national-
team/2010/08/us-falls-to-brazil−2−0.aspx.

Wilson, Jeremy. "David Luiz: I turned to God when I was dropped by Jose Mourinho at Chelsea." The Telegraph. Sept. 25, 2013. http://www.telegraph.co.uk/sport/football/teams/chelsea/10334798/David-Luiz-I-turned-to-God-when-I-was-dropped-by-Jose-Mourinho-at-Chelsea.html.

Toward the Goal, Revised Edition

The Kaká Story

Jeremy V. Jones

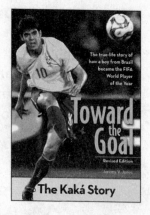

"I learned that it is faith that decides whether something will happen or not." At the age of eight, Kaká already knew what he wanted in life: to play soccer and only soccer. He started playing in front of his friends and family, but after a crippling injury, doctors told him he would never play again. Through faith and perseverance Kaká recovered and has since become a FIFA World Player of the Year and winner of the Ballon d'Or. This updated edition tells the story of the midfielder for Real Madrid who has become one of the most recognized faces on the soccer field.

Available in stores and online!

Linspired

The Jeremy Lin Story

Mike Yorkey with Jesse Florea

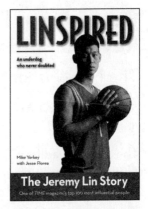

No athletic scholarships, ignored by the NBA draft, waived by team after team, yet Jeremy Lin remained positive and never doubted God's plan. Finally picked up by the New York Knicks, a teammate's injury placed Lin on the court after weeks on the bench. Since then, Lin has captivated the sports world with his incredible basketball skills as a New York Knick and now Houston Rocket. This is his remarkable story.

Available in stores and online!

Defender of Faith, Revised Edition

The Mike Fisher Story

Kim Washburn

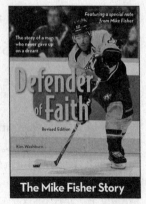

The revised edition of *Defender of Faith* describes the extraordinary true story of professional hockey player Mike Fisher, who grew up to become one of the NHL's greatest stars and is now married to country singer Carrie Underwood. He has been nominated for the Selke Trophy as the best defensive forward in the league, he's competed in the Stanley Cup finals, and he's been a former alternate captain for the Ottawa Senators. Today he plays professionally for the Nashville Predators and is an active humanitarian, using his fame to benefit others and putting his faith in Christ first—both on and off the ice.

Available in stores and online!

ZONDERVAN®
.com

Driven by Faith

The Trevor Bayne Story

Godwin Kelly

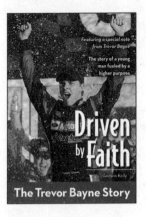

Embracing the Race Trevor Bayne is
the youngest race car driver ever to
win the Daytona 500. Throughout his
high-speed career, from his early start
driving go-karts to his incredible win
at NASCAR's biggest race, Trevor attributes all his success to
God—both on and off the track. His amazing story, from start
to finish, will inspire young and old, racing enthusiasts or not, as
they read *Driven by Faith*, the story of a boy unafraid to share
his faith and a man who gives all the glory to God. Includes a
personal note from Trevor Bayne.

Available in stores and online!